W9-ADQ-930

INNOVATORS

The Beatles

British Pop Sensation

STUART A. KALLEN

KIDHAVEN PRESS
A part of Gale, Cengage Learning

GALE
CENGAGE Learning™

Detroit • New York • San Francisco • New Haven, Conn • Waterville, Maine • London

© 2011 Gale, Cengage Learning

LIBRARY OF CONGRESS CATALOGING-IN-PUBLICATION DATA

Kallen, Stuart A., 1955-
The Beatles : British pop sensation / by Stuart Kallen.
 p. cm. -- (Innovators)
Includes bibliographical references and index.
ISBN 978-0-7377-5868-9 (hardcover)
1. Beatles--Juvenile literature. 2. Rock musicians--England--Biography--Juvenile literature. I. Title.
ML3930.B39K35 2011
782.42166092'2--dc22
[B]
                                                                    2011005786

KidHaven Press
27500 Drake Rd.
Farmington Hills, MI 48331

ISBN-13: 978-0-7377-5868-9
ISBN-10: 0-7377-5868-6

Printed in the United States of America
1 2 3 4 5 6 7 15 14 13 12 11

Printed by Bang Printing, Brainerd, MN, 1st Ptg., 06/2011

CONTENTS

Greatest Artists of All Time

In June 2010 the music magazine *Rolling Stone* named the Beatles number one in their list of the "Greatest Artists of All Time." The British rock group, together from 1962 to 1970, topped a list that included the world's 100 most influential performers, including rock icons Elvis Presley, the Rolling Stones, and Michael Jackson.

Every Record was a Shock

The Beatles were the world's top rock group by the time they broke up in 1970. More than 40 years after their demise, millions of people still listen to the Beatles every day. Many feel the group's music is as fresh and vital as the day it was created. From the time they released their first **album** in 1963, their music was so creative and original, famous songwriter Elvis Costello writes, "Every record was a shock when it came out…. the Beatles arrived sounding like nothing else."[1]

The Beatles surprised listeners. They wrote complex and unique songs with memorable melodies and words. The group's fantastic vocal harmonies could be raw and soulful or soothing and angelic. And the band merged many musical styles, including 1920s dance hall, country, rhythm and blues, and rock and roll. Throughout their recording career, the Beatles never repeated themselves. Their inventive songs were recorded with unusual sound effects that had never been heard before in rock music.

The innovative, influential music created by the Beatles (from left, Paul McCartney, John Lennon, Ringo Starr, and George Harrison) remains vital more than 40 years after their breakup.

No other group can compare to the Beatles when it comes to selling records, and they were much more than just a groundbreaking band. From the moment they gained widespread popularity in 1963, the Beatles influenced not only music but fashion, films, and culture. The group created the first music videos. They also inspired millions of men to grow long hair and wear pointy "Beatle boots" and round, wire-rimmed glasses. Throughout the 1960s, during the era of the **hippies**, the Beatles were hippest of all. Without the Beatles, the revolutionary sixties would not have been the same. The group provided a soundtrack filled with innovative and unique music that remains unmatched decades after it was recorded.

CHAPTER 1

Becoming the Fab Four

Every weekday in the early 1960s, the Cavern Club in Liverpool, England, attracted hundreds of people on their lunch breaks. The Cavern was in a windowless underground tunnel where the brick walls oozed foul brown water that dripped from the streets above. The air was blue with cigarette smoke. No one went to the Cavern Club to eat. The office workers, schoolgirls, and secretaries went to the Cavern in the middle of the day to dance to the Beatles. The four boys in the band were crammed onto a tiny stage at one end of the tunnel. They played so loudly that the music bounced off the filthy walls like gunfire.

At night the Cavern stage hosted slick jazz musicians. The Beatles were totally unlike those rehearsed bands. Guitarists John Lennon and George Harrison, bass player Paul McCartney, and drummer Ringo Starr were fun and informal. Rather than following a list of songs, the Beatles launched into songs shouted out by audience members. Most requests were for

The Beatles (from left, Harrison, McCartney, Starr, and Lennon) perform at the Cavern Club in Liverpool, England, in 1962. Their sets at the time were largely made up of covers of songs made famous by American rock and roll stars.

American rock and roll numbers by Elvis Presley, Little Richard, Chuck Berry, and Gene Vincent. Lead vocalist Lennon often forgot the lyrics, so he made up his own. These verses were often filled with puns, jokes, and obscene rhymes. But when the group got serious, it was obvious that the Beatles were the tightest, most talented band around. The Cavern owners agreed. The Beatles were hired to play 292 shows, or gigs, in the underground club between February 21, 1961, and August 2, 1963.

By the time the Beatles played their last gig at the Cavern, they were one of the top groups in England. Although they were considered an overnight sensation, the band had been working hard to develop their talents for more than five years.

Nothing but "Rock 'n' Roll"

The roots of the Beatles can be traced to a church picnic in Liverpool on July 6, 1957. Sixteen-year-old John Lennon played his first gig at the church with his group the Quarrymen. Lennon was strongly influenced by Elvis Presley's "Heartbreak Hotel," which was a huge hit in Britain. As Lennon later remembered: "Once I heard [Elvis] and got into it, that was life, there was no other thing. I thought of nothing else but rock 'n' roll."[2]

After the first Quarrymen show, a friend introduced Lennon to guitarist Paul McCartney, who was only fourteen. Although he was younger, McCartney was a talented musician who impressed Lennon with his singing and playing. Before long, McCartney was asked to join the Quarrymen as a guitarist. In February 1958, McCartney brought George Harrison, barely fourteen years old, into the group as lead guitarist. Pete Best was hired to played drums. The Quarrymen changed their name to the Silver Beatles for a time and then settled on the Beatles. Lennon chose the insect-based name because his favorite band was Buddy Holly and the Crickets.

In 1960 the Beatles—made up of Lennon, McCartney, Harrison, Best, and bass player Stu Sutcliffe—traveled to Hamburg, Germany, where they played in various clubs for up to eight hours a day. Club owners expected the Beatles to keep things exciting so the crowds would not wander off. One nightclub owner told the group in German, to *mak show*, or make a show. For the Beatles, making a show meant stretching out two-minute rock songs with long improvised guitar solos and choruses

in three-part harmony. As Lennon later recalled, "Every number lasted about 20 minutes…. We had to try even harder, put our heart and soul into it…. The Germans loved it."[3]

Bigger Than Elvis

The Beatles returned to Liverpool in 1962. By this time, Sutcliffe had left the group, and Ringo Starr, whose real name was Richard Starkey, had replaced Best on the drums. The group also had a new manager, Brian Epstein. He visited every record company in London. Epstein could not interest anyone in the Beatles. Dick Rowe, an executive at Decca Records, famously told the Beatles'

After forming as the Quarrymen a few years earlier, by 1960 the band had a new name and five members (from left, Pete Best, Harrison, Lennon, McCartney, and Stu Sutcliffe). The Beatles gained an early following playing clubs in Hamburg, Germany, where this photo was taken.

manager, "Guitar groups are on the way out, Mr. Epstein."[4] Epstein angrily replied that the Beatles would someday be bigger than Elvis Presley.

In early 1963 Epstein finally convinced Parlophone EMI to sign the Beatles to a recording contract. George Martin, a Parlophone record **producer** and arranger, made that decision. Martin went on to produce every Beatles album but one.

After recording a **single**, "Love Me Do," with the Beatles, Martin booked the studio to record a fourteen-song, LP (long-playing) album. Because the Beatles were a rookie band with a very small recording budget, they had to record the LP live in a single session. To achieve this, the Beatles simply played their live stage show in the studio.

Unlike modern recording artists who spend months in the studio, the Beatles recorded their first album in only 9 hours and 45 minutes. The quick recording

Brian Epstein took over as the Beatles' manager in 1962 and gained the band its first recording contract with Parlophone EMI in 1963.

method successfully captured the party atmosphere of their live shows. As Lennon states, the record "was the nearest thing to what we might have sounded like to audiences in Hamburg and Liverpool."[5]

Please Please Me

The Beatles' first album, *Please Please Me,* has eight songs that Lennon and McCartney wrote together and six cover tunes written by others. The album kicks off with the Lennon/McCartney song "I Saw Her Standing There." McCartney counts off one, two, three, four, and the driving rhythm and handclaps instantly create a catchy dance beat. The soaring, seamless, three-part harmonies show off the band's flair for singing.

The innovative talent of the Beatles is obvious on the album's other songs. Slow, melodic Lennon/McCartney tunes such as "Do You Want to Know a Secret?" and "There's a Place" show that the band can do more than play hard-driving rock and roll. These were sincere, pleasant-sounding songs that even parents could love.

Upon its release on March 22, *Please Please Me* immediately went to the top of the LP charts printed in the *New Musical Express* (NME), Britain's leading music magazine. The album remained number one for a record-breaking 30 weeks along with several Lennon/McCartney singles from the album, "Please Please Me" and "From Me to You."

McCartney, Harrison, Starr, producer George Martin, and Lennon display an award for selling 250,000 copies of the Beatles' first album, *Please Please Me,* only three weeks after its release in March 1963.

The Beatles started out as a rowdy bar band that did not play by the formal rules of show business. They sharpened their talents through countless hours onstage and quickly surpassed their musical peers. Their songwriting skills helped make an instant hit of their debut album. It was obvious to anyone who listened that John, Paul, George, and Ringo were the Fab Four, their fabulous new nickname given to them by fans.

CHAPTER 2

Beatlemania

In June 1963 the Beatles were still playing regularly at the Cavern Club, but their fan base was growing. Even before their next single had a name, thousands of people placed advance orders for the song at record stores. By the time "She Loves You" was released at the end of August, there were 500,000 advance orders for the song. "She Loves You" instantly went to number one on the New Music Express charts. "She Loves You" quickly took the title as the biggest selling single in British history, remaining on the music charts for 31 weeks total.

When "She Loves You" was released, the song proved that the Beatles' writing and playing skills were growing. The high harmonies on the "yeah, yeah, yeah" chorus gave the song a strong memorable melody, called a *hook*. It was easy for teenagers to sing, it sounded great in the car, and anyone could dance to it. Moreover, the wit, charm, and sweetness of the Beatles came through in the music.

Fan Frenzy

On October 13 the Beatles performed on the top-rated British TV show, *Sunday Night at the London Palladium*. From the first seconds that the band played "From Me to You," the teenage girls in the audience shrieked uncontrollably. Some even fainted.

More than 15 million viewers saw the Beatles on their first TV performance, but it was the scene outside the theater that made headlines. Thousands of teenage girls arrived at the Palladium hours before the band was scheduled to play. Fans screamed, chanted the names of band members and piled up a mountain of written notes, candy, and gifts in front of the stage

London police hold back screaming Beatles fans outside the Palladium before an October 1963 appearance. The media coined the word *Beatlemania* to describe the frenzied behavior of the band's followers.

Beatlemania made fans eager to collect anything featuring their idols, including lunch boxes, pins, photos, scarves, photographs, and other items that often had nothing to do with music.

doors. The scene attracted reporters, and the following day every newspaper in Great Britain featured stories about the chaos around the Palladium. The *Daily Mirror* newspaper coined a new word, **Beatlemania**, to describe the intense fan frenzy.

It was a Zoo

Throughout the closing months of 1963, the Beatles played a series of shows in Great Britain. Beatlemania followed the group everywhere they went. In Plymouth a rowdy crowd of Beatles fans outside a theater started a riot. Interest in the band was so high that when McCartney caught the flu in Portsmouth, radio stations gave hour-by-hour updates on the bass player's condition.

At some shows unruly fans stormed the stage, trying to tear the band's clothes and yank out strands of their hair. Starr remembers a scary event in Paris: "It was like being in a zoo on stage! It felt dangerous. The kids were out of hand. It was the first time I felt that if they got near us we would be ripped apart."[6]

Beyond the concert hall, Beatlemania influenced fashion everywhere in Britain. Manufactures produced pointy Beatle boots and collarless Beatles jackets like those worn by the band. London wig factories worked around the clock to produce Beatle "moptop" wigs. Other Beatles products included lunch boxes, bubblegum cards, purses, clocks, and stamps. Never before had any music stars been promoted in this manner. People even began to speak like the Beatles, using Liverpool slang words such as "gear" for great, "grotty" for gross, and "groovy" for good.

Conquering America

In early November, EMI announced that the next Beatles single, "I Want to Hold Your Hand," had sold a million advance copies, a first in British recording history. When "I Want to Hold Your Hand" was released on November 29, it instantly climbed to number one, knocking "She Loves You," out of the number one position.

In early December, a radio disc jockey in Washington, D.C., played a copy of "I Want to Hold Your Hand" he had picked up in London. Within minutes, listeners began phoning the station requesting the song. Its release in the United States on

Media and security surround the Beatles as they wave to fans after their arrival at New York's Kennedy Airport in February 1964 for their first trip to the United States.

December 25 began the American Beatlemania. The band was covered in newspapers and magazines, and on TV and radio.

"She Loves You" was released in the United States in January, and it went to Number One on the *Billboard* magazine charts. When the popular *Ed Sullivan Show* announced that the

The Beatles appear on the set of *The Ed Sullivan Show* with host Ed Sullivan, left, in February 1964. Their performance on the program, their first U.S. television appearance, was watched by more than 73 million Americans.

Beatles would appear in February, the show received 50,000 ticket requests for the 700-seat theater.

When the Beatles' airplane landed at New York's Kennedy Airport on February 7, 1964, 5,000 screaming fans were there to greet them. Lennon recalled the scene: "They're wild; they're all wild. They just all seem out of their minds."[7] Two nights later, more than 73 million Americans—almost half the country—watched the Beatles on *The Ed Sullivan Show*. In the following days, the Beatles played their first American concerts. More than 6 million ticket requests poured in for two concerts at the 3,000-seat Carnegie Hall in New York City.

In April 1964 the Beatles broke more sales records. All of the top five *Billboard* best-sellers were Beatles songs. In addition, the group had fourteen singles in the Top 100.

A Hard Day's Night

Beatlemania was perfectly captured in the band's first movie, *A Hard Day's Night,* which premiered in June 1964. In an era before MTV, the Internet, and cable TV, the movie gave fans an inside look at their favorite band for the first time. Like the group's music, *A Hard Day's Night* set a new standard for films. It also turned the Beatles into overnight movie stars.

Many critics consider *A Hard Day's Night* to be the most original rock and roll movie ever made. It is filmed in a black-

The Beatles' first movie, *A Hard Day's Night*, released in 1964, captures the band's experiences at the height of Beatlemania.

and-white documentary style and shows a typical day in the life of the Beatles during the height of Beatlemania. The band is chased through the streets by fans and mobbed at a train station. They play "She Loves You" before an audience of mostly girls, who scream without pause and jump up and down with tears running down their faces.

A Hard Day's Night showed that the Beatles were funny, fashionable, and sassy as well as sweet. The film also intensified Beatlemania and created an intense worldwide love for a rock group that has rarely been duplicated. The Beatles were new, they looked and sounded completely different, and rock and roll would never be the same.

CHAPTER 3

Celebrity and Controversy

By 1965 the Beatles were the most famous people in the world, and everyone knew them as John, Paul, George, and Ringo. The group was selling millions of records, and they played sold-out shows in the United States, Europe, Hong Kong, Australia, and New Zealand. Even though no member of the group was over 25 years old, presidents, kings, politicians, and movie stars all wanted to meet the Beatles.

Bob Dylan's Influence

Even as Beatlemania continued at full force, the band was changing and growing. This was partially due to a influential new voice in popular music, American singer and songwriter Bob Dylan. In July 1965 Dylan's song "Like a Rolling Stone" was the number two song in the country behind "Help!" by the Beatles.

Dylan's song was unlike anything else on the radio at the time. The gravelly-voiced singer was critical of the world. He wrote complex, wordy lyrics about phony people, prejudice, and war. Whereas the Beatles wrote catchy three-minute love songs, Dylan songs, such as "Like a Rolling Stone," "Mr. Tambourine Man," and "It's All Right, Ma (I'm Only Bleeding)," were more than six minutes long.

The Beatles idolized Dylan, and he influenced the group in two ways. Musically, the Beatles started writing more poetic, personal, and inward-looking songs. This was seen in Lennon compositions such as "In My Life" and "You've Got to Hide Your Love Away." As Lennon explained: "I'd started thinking about my own emotions.... I would try to express what I felt about myself.... It was Dylan who helped me."[8] Dylan was also the first person to expose the Beatles to marijuana—a drug with a long history of use among musicians. Marijuana is said to intensify the musical experience. Although the drug has negative effects, such as short-term memory loss, it influenced the Beatles' songwriting and recording experiences.

Musicians such as the Beatles and Dylan were not the only people smoking marijuana in the mid-1960s.

Iconic American folk singer and songwriter Bob Dylan influenced the Beatles to begin writing and recording more poetic, introspective songs.

The Beatles perform in August 1965 to 55,000 fans at New York's Shea Stadium — the first time a rock concert was held in a sports stadium.

At the time, the hippie movement was sweeping across the Western world. Millions of young people were experimenting with the drug. This was a new development among the white, middle-class hippies who formed the roots of the counterculture.

Help!

As early as 1965, the Beatles were seen as the leaders of the hippie movement, and they were as popular as ever. Their second movie, *Help!*, was a spoof on James Bond spy movies. When *Help!* premiered, the film and the soundtrack album sold extremely well, and the group continued to break sales records.

When the Beatles played Shea Stadium in New York on August 15, more than 55,000 people attended. It was the first rock concert held in a stadium. By the late 1960s, nearly every major band was playing baseball stadiums, but the Beatles were the first to do so.

Hearing New Sounds

When the Beatles released *Rubber Soul* in December 1965, it was the

Harrison plays the sitar, a traditional stringed instrument from India, while sitting with a teacher and the other band members in 1966. The Beatles experimented with unusual sounds and instruments not normally heard on rock and roll records, using the sitar to carry the melody of Rubber Soul's "Norwegian Wood."

group's sixth album in three years. Although they had been touring the world almost nonstop, the group continued to reinvent their music in the studio. Harrison commented that on *Rubber Soul* "we were suddenly hearing sounds that we weren't able to hear before."[9]

The new sounds on *Rubber Soul* included a traditional instrument from India never before used on a rock and roll record. In the song "Norwegian Wood," Harrison plucks out the melody on a **sitar**. Several critics credit Harrison for introducing non-Western musical influences to rock and roll. This helped lay the foundation for what would later be called world music.

The rest of the unique sounds on *Rubber Soul* include acoustic guitars, jangling electric guitars, distorted "fuzz tone" bass, and a harpsichord-like piano. The meaning behind many of the songs on *Rubber Soul* was also different from that of most traditional rock albums. In "The Word," for instance, Lennon sings that everyone should say the word *love*, because it will set them free. This song of love in the universal sense, rather than in the romantic sense, was a new message in rock music.

Recording the crafted, layered sound of *Rubber Soul* took much more time than previous Beatles' albums, which were recorded as quickly as possible. Sessions for *Rubber Soul* often stretched past midnight, and the album took more than a month to record. Although long recording sessions soon became commonplace for major bands, the Beatles were pioneers in this.

Thousands of Monks Chanting

The Beatles' next album, *Revolver,* was a new achievement in musical experimentation and took even longer to record. Like *Rubber Soul,* the new album was heavily influenced by drugs. In late 1965 Lennon and Harrison were given a **psychedelic** drug known as LSD (lysergic acid diethylamide) by their dentist.

LSD, also called acid, was legal in 1965. Like marijuana, many hippies were experimenting with the drug. LSD is much more powerful than marijuana. It makes people hallucinate—see and hear things that are not real—and can influence the way people perceive the world. People who take LSD sometimes "hear colors" or "taste sounds." LSD can also cause extremely bad experiences in which users scream, cry, and have suicidal thoughts.

Lennon took a lot of LSD in early 1966, and the drug's effects caused him to write music that was very different. When recording sessions for *Revolver* began on April 6, 1966, Lennon worked to create sounds he heard while high on LSD. These were unlike any other noises ever put on recording tape.

The song "Tomorrow Never Knows" was meant to reflect the LSD experience. The lyrics were inspired by the *Tibetan Book of the Dead*. This ancient religious text describes the Tibetan belief in the afterlife. No other rock song had discussed such deep concepts, and Lennon wanted the music to sound like "thousands of monks chanting."[10] To achieve this, the Beatles filled the song with backward guitar parts, distortion, electronic sounds, and unconventional musical instruments.

Not every song on *Revolver* was as weighty as "Tomorrow Never Knows." "Yellow Submarine," inspired by Lennon's first LSD trip, is a light, happy song. It features Starr singing over glasses clinking, party chatter, and Lennon blowing bubbles in a bucket through a straw.

The End of Touring

In 1966 the Beatles' record company wanted the group to leave the studio for another world tour to promote their new music. This tour was filled with danger and controversy. Problems began in March 1966, when Lennon told an interviewer that the Beatles are "more popular than Jesus now."[11] The comment appeared in the American teen magazine *Datebook*. Lennon's comment created outrage in the United States two weeks before the Beatles were about to begin their extended tour. In the southern states,

Teenagers in Georgia protest against Lennon's comment that the Beatles were "more popular than Jesus now" by burning the band's records and photographs at a rally in 1966.

protesters held anti-Beatle demonstrations in several cities. Urged on by radio disc jockeys, people attended events where they burned Beatles records in huge public bonfires. Thirty-five radio stations banned Beatles music. Lennon apologized, but hate mail and death threats arrived at Beatles headquarters daily.

In August 1966 the Beatles played Candlestick Park in San Francisco. After more than 1,400 live shows, this was to be the last concert performance for the world's most famous band. As Lennon later said: "We've had enough of performing forever. I can't imagine any reason which would make us do any sort of tour again. We're all really tired. It does nothing for us anymore."[12]

Fans were stunned when the Beatles stopped touring. The band's innovations had completely transformed rock music in the space of a few years, but now Beatlemania was over.

CHAPTER 4

Revolutionary Sounds

After the Beatles' last concert tour in the summer of 1966, Lennon went to Spain to film a movie, *How I Won the War*. In Spain Lennon was isolated from the Beatles for the first time in years. Sad, alone, and reflecting on his future, he wrote a song, "Strawberry Fields Forever." The song would send the Beatles in a new direction and lead to a creative phase that changed rock music forever.

Way Ahead of Its Time

Strawberry Fields was the name of an orphanage near Lennon's boyhood home in Liverpool. A beautiful garden party was held there each summer. The lyrics of "Strawberry Fields Forever" blend Lennon's happy memories of his youth with observations about his life as an artist.

The musical production of "Strawberry Fields Forever" was time-consuming and extremely complex. The dreamlike song is composed of several dozen different "takes," or performances, equal to 42 minutes of music. These sounds are layered together into a four-minute, ten-second song. Instruments include a primitive electric **synthesizer** called a Mellotron and recorded drum cymbals played backwards. The sound is tinted with trumpets, cellos, and a stringed Indian instrument called a **swarmandal**, played by Harrison. Martin later said that "Strawberry Fields Forever" was "way ahead of its time… [a] work of an undoubted genius… the most original and inventive track to date in pop music."[13]

"Strawberry Fields Forever" was released as a single in March 1967. To promote the song, the Beatles produced the first stand-alone music video, which was later shown on TV. The film of the Beatles fooling around with a decorated piano by a tree uses backward shots and distorted imagery.

While showing off a new song, the "Strawberry Fields Forever" video also showed the world new Beatles fashions. Everyone in the group now had mustaches and layered shag haircuts, and Lennon wore a pair of round, wire-framed glasses. Within weeks the hairstyles and facial hair were seen on young people everywhere. Round, wire-rimmed glasses, which had gone out of style in the 1920s, have been worn by millions of people for decades since.

Sgt. Pepper's Band

When "Strawberry Fields Forever" was released, the Beatles were already busy recording their next album, *Sgt. Pepper's Lonely Hearts Club Band*. From December 6, 1966, until April 20, 1967, the Beatles spent countless hours creating unusual sound effects in the studio. At one point Lennon even asked to be sus-

McCartney takes to the podium to conduct members of the London Symphony Orchestra in February 1967 during the recording of "A Day in the Life" for *Sgt. Pepper's Lonely Hearts Club Band.*

pended from the studio ceiling above a microphone with a rope tied around his waist. He wanted to get a shifting vocal sound while twirling dizzily in a rapid circle. This technique for obtaining a one-of-a-kind vocal performance was considered too dangerous by Martin and never attempted. Instead, the Beatles used instruments not traditionally used in rock music to achieve exceptional sounds.

Harrison's song "Within You and Without You" was recorded with Indian musicians playing traditional instruments, including the sitar, swarmandal, and small hand drums called tabla drums. To achieve a carnival sound on the song "Being for the Benefit of Mr. Kite," the group made multiple recordings of **calliopes** and organs. They chopped up the recording tapes with scissors, threw them in the air, and randomly taped the pieces back together. This provided an unusual swirling psychedelic sound. On "A Day in the Life," 41 members of the

London Symphony Orchestra play a noisy, free-form finale that builds to a thundering peak.

A Concept Album

Sgt. Pepper's was the first rock "concept" album with songs based on a single unifying theme. The idea was McCartney's. He set it up as if John, Paul, George, and Ringo were members of a totally different group—*Sgt. Pepper's Lonely Hearts Club Band.*

The iconic cover of *Sgt. Pepper's Lonely Hearts Club Band* features two incarnations of the band members as well as cutout images of other celebrities.

The album cover was one of the first to open to double size and to have song lyrics printed on it. Band members appeared in brightly colored, satin military uniforms next to wax dummies of the old Beatles from the "She Loves You" era. They were surrounded by cardboard cutouts of celebrities, such as actress Mae West, writer Edgar Allan Poe, and even Bob Dylan.

Sgt. Pepper's was released on June 1, 1967, and the psychedelic sounds on the album made it an instant success. By August, 2.5 million copies were sold. The album remains among the most beloved of all Beatles albums. In 2003 *Rolling Stone* magazine ranked *Sgt. Pepper's* No. 1 of the 500 Greatest Albums of All Time.

A Stripped-Down Sound

Even as critical praise for *Sgt. Pepper's* reached a peak, the Beatles had once again moved in a different direction. While dozens of other rock groups were trying to imitate the sound and look of *Sgt. Pepper's,* the Beatles abandoned their complex psychedelic sounds. Their next album, released in November 1968, featured a stripped-down musical approach. The title and cover were totally different. The album was simply called *The Beatles,* but came to be known as *The White Album* because of its stark white cover.

The White Album is actually two LPs with 30 songs in total. Many of the songs pay a mocking tribute to various types of pop music. The first song, "Back in the U.S.S.R.," has harmonies that mimic the surf music made popular by the Beach Boys. "Rocky Raccoon" is a spoof on the folksy **ballads** found on Dylan's *John Wesley Harding* album. *The White Album* also featured extremely inventive songs. "Helter Skelter" and "Everybody's Got Something to Hide Except Me and My Monkey" inspired punk

McCartney and Lennon harmonize during a studio recording session in February 1968. After the psychedelic complexity of *Sgt. Pepper's*, the band sought a simpler sound for their next album, officially titled *The Beatles* but known as *The White Album*.

music a decade later. And Lennon's "Revolution 9," more than eight minutes long, consists of 30 tapes of sound effects layered upon one another. Lennon was fascinated with the experimental music, saying: "*This* is the music of the future.... You can forget all the rest of the [stuff] we've done—this is *it!*" [14]

Let It Be

Despite Lennon's enthusiasm, the Beatles were falling apart after years of intense musical work. Band members could barely stand to be in the same room together. McCartney did not want the

The Beatles perform on the roof of Apple Records in January 1969 for the documentary *Let It Be*. This was their last public concert; by the next year, the band had broken up.

band to break up, so he organized a final album in September 1969. *Abbey Road* was the Beatles' eleventh studio album in six-and-a-half years.

Abbey Road features the Beatles at their finest. Songs such as Harrison's "Here Comes the Sun" and McCartney's "You Never Give Me Your Money" helped make *Abbey Road* the band's best-selling album to date. But when the band recorded Lennon's "I Want You (She's So Heavy)" on August 20, 1969, it was the last time all four Beatles were together in a studio.

On September 20, 1969, Lennon quit the Beatles but did not tell the press. On April 10, 1970, McCartney gave a press conference in which he announced he was leaving the band. A few weeks later, the film *Let It Be* was released. Shot in early

1969, it showed the Beatles, tired and bored, working on songs in the studio together. Critics panned the movie, but millions went to see *Let It Be* to view last moments of their favorite band playing together.

The Beatles Will Live Forever

The Beatles were the best-selling artists of the 1960s. During the eight years of their recording career, they were number one on the weekly record charts one-third of the time. The group influenced almost every rock musician and pop group, including the Rolling Stones, Pink Floyd, Led Zeppelin, and Jimi Hendrix. It is safe to say that the 1960s would have sounded entirely different without the Beatles. The group also changed how people looked, talked, acted, and played.

An iTunes card featuring the Beatles promotes the online launch of the band's entire catalog of music on Apple's iTunes Store in November 2010.

After the Beatles broke up, John, Paul, George, and Ringo each began solo careers with varying levels of success. Tragically, Lennon was murdered in 1980, devastating millions and insuring that there would never be a Beatles reunion. The group produced enough music to fill sixteen CDs. These were digitally remixed and released in a boxed set on September 9, 2009. When the set came out, the Beatles once again broke numerous sales records. More than 2.25 million CDs were purchased within five days. In November 2010 the entire catalog of the Beatles songs was offered on Apple's online iTunes Store for the first time. During the first week, more than 2 million individual songs and 450,000 Beatles albums were downloaded from the digital media store. These sales figures topped new releases by twenty-first-century superstars such as Taylor Swift and Eminem.

These Beatles offerings will likely influence a new generation. On CDs, MP3s, and in the sounds made by millions of other musicians, the Beatles will live forever in music.

Notes

Introduction: Greatest Artists of All Time

1. Elvis Costello. "The Beatles." *Rolling Stone*, June 2010. www
.rollingstone.com/music/lists/5702/31963/31964.

Chapter 1: Becoming the Fab Four

2. Quoted in The Beatles. *The Beatles Anthology*. San Francisco:
Chronicle Books, 2000, p. 11.
3. Quoted in Hunter Davies. *The Beatles*. New York: W.W.
Norton, 2002, p. 122.
4. Quoted in Chris Gregory. *Who Could Ask for More?: Reclaim-
ing the Beatles*. London: The Plotted Plain Press, 2008, p.
35.
5. Quoted in The Beatles. *The Beatles Anthology*, p. 92.

Chapter 2: Beatlemania

6. The Beatles. *The Beatles Anthology*, p. 106.
7. The Beatles. *The Beatles Anthology*, p. 119.

Chapter 3: Celebrity and Controversy

8. Quoted in Jann S. Wenner. *Lennon Remembers*. New York:
Rolling Stone Press, 2000, pp. 83–84.
9. The Beatles. *The Beatles Anthology*, p. 194.
10. Quoted in Walter Everett. *The Beatles As Musicians: "Revolver" through the Anthology*. Oxford: Oxford University
Press, 1999, p. 35.
11. Quoted in Everett. *The Beatles As Musicians*, p. 70.
12. The Beatles. *The Beatles Anthology*, p. 229.

Chapter 4: Revolutionary Sounds

13. George Martin. *With a Little Help from My Friends: The Making of Sgt. Pepper*. New York: Little, Brown and Company,
1994, p. 24.
14. Quoted in Pete Shotten and Nicholas Schaffner. *John Lennon: In My Life*. New York: Stein and Day, 1983, p. 176.

GLOSSARY

album: During the Beatle era, an album was a 12-inch (30 cm) vinyl, long-playing (LP) record that could hold about twenty minutes of music on each side.

ballad: A song with lyrics that tell a story.

Beatlemania: The intense fan frenzy directed toward the Beatles.

calliope: An automatic, steam-powered organ invented in the nineteenth century, often installed in carousels or merry-go-rounds.

hippie: A term used to define members of a youth movement that began in San Francisco in the mid-1960s. Hippies experimented with drugs, such as marijuana and LSD, and popularized health foods, environmentalism, music festivals, and the antiwar movement.

producer: In music, a producer works with a band to manage and oversee the recording process. Producer George Martin helped the Beatles create innovative sounds and also created orchestral arrangements for the band.

psychedelic: A word used to describe the effect of the drug LSD, from Greek words that mean to *manifest the soul* or *mind-manifesting*.

single: A 7-inch (17.7 cm) vinyl record with a single song on each side.

sitar: A complex instrument used in Hindustani classical music with 21 to 23 strings and moveable frets.

swarmandal: An Indian harp, about 30 inches (76 cm) long and 15 inches (38 cm) wide with 21 to 36 strings. George Harrison used the instrument in several Beatles songs, including "Strawberry Fields Forever."

synthesizer: An electronic instrument, usually played with a keyboard, that produces complex sounds that mimic other instruments such as violins and horns.

FOR FURTHER EXPLORATION

Books

Jennifer Joline Anderson. *John Lennon: Legendary Musician & Beatle.* Edina, MN: Abdo Publishing Company, 2010. A biography of John Lennon that covers his life from his boyhood in Liverpool through his Beatles years to his tragic death at age 40 in 1980.

Gary Berman. *We're Going to See the Beatles.* Santa Monica: Santa Monica Press, 2008. An oral history of Beatlemania as told by fans who attended Beatles concerts between 1963 and 1966.

Jim Gallagher. *The Beatles.* Broomall, PA: Mason Crest Publishers, 2007. This book explores the individual lives of each Beatle to help readers understand what influenced the band and their art.

Saddleback Educational Publishing. *The Beatles: Graphic Biography.* Irvine, CA: Three Watson, 2008. A fast-paced and easy-to-read history of the Beatles with an emphasis on the group's pioneering music, published in full-color comic book style.

Websites

Paul McCartney (www.paulmccartney.com). In 2011 the bass player and songwriter was still making music, producing albums, touring, and singing Beatles songs in concert. This site features materials about McCartney's productive solo years.

The Beatles (www.beatles.com). The official Beatles website with information about every song, album, film, and video; also includes articles, history, and dozens of photographs.

INDEX

Picture Credits

ABOUT THE AUTHOR

Stuart A. Kallen is the author of more than 250 nonfiction books for children and young adults. He has written on topics ranging from the theory of relativity to the history of rock and roll. In addition, Mr. Kallen has written award-winning children's videos and television scripts. In his spare time, he is a singer/songwriter/guitarist in San Diego.